May

by Mari Kesselring
Illustrated by Brian Caleb Dumm

Content Consultant:
Susan Kesselring, MA
Literacy Educator and Preschool Director

visit us at www.abdopublishing.com

Published by Magic Wagon, a division of the ABDO Group, 8000 West 78th Street, Edina, Minnesota 55439. Copyright © 2010 by Abdo Consulting Group, Inc. International copyrights reserved in all countries. All rights reserved. No part of this book may be reproduced in any form without written permission from the publisher.

Looking Glass Library™ is a trademark and logo of Magic Wagon.

Printed in the United States.

 PRINTED ON RECYCLED PAPER

Text by Mari Kesselring
Illustrations by Brian Caleb Dumm
Edited by Patricia Stockland
Interior layout and design by Emily Love
Cover design by Emily Love

Library of Congress Cataloging-in-Publication Data

Kesselring, Mari.
  May / by Mari Kesselring ; illustrated by Brian Caleb Dumm ; content consultant,
      Susan Kesselring.
    p. cm. — (Months of the year)
  ISBN 978-1-60270-632-3
  1. May (Month)—Juvenile literature. 2. Calendar—Juvenile literature. I. Dumm,
Brian Caleb, ill. II. Kesselring, Susan. III. Title.
  CE13.K479 2010
  398'.33—dc22

                       2008050698

What is the month
between April and June?
Hurry up!
Give me an answer soon!

MoM ♥

I can't hear you.

What did you say?

You're right! Well done!

The answer is May!

Wow!

There are 31 days in May.

Let's learn about this

month's special ways.

May is National Hamburger Month.

How perfect for grilling!

Make your own hamburger

tasty and filling.

Lawn bowling is a fun game
that needs no sticks or net.
Invite your friends to play.
Don't forget your pet!

Cinco de Mayo on May 5
is a day for fun—
for Mexican friends
and everyone.

Walk your dog. Feed your cat.
Shine your bird's beak.
The second week of May
is named Pet Week!

Pickle

Kitty

Some moms really
like May a lot.
Mother's Day is in May,
in case you forgot.

On Armed Forces Day
we think of military people who serve.
We show them the respect
and honor they deserve.

ARMED FORCES DAY

The third Sunday in May
is called Peace Day.
We learn to be kind
in what we do and say.

May is over now,
but don't you worry.
June is coming
in a hurry!

SHINGTON
EMENTARY
SCHOOL

23

Peaceful Plans

Think about ways that you and your family can live a peaceful life. Have a parent help you make a list of peaceful activities for your family. You could plant flowers in your yard or listen to soft music together. Hang up the list in your house. When you are looking for something to do, check the list!

Make Up a Pet!

Celebrate Pet Week! During the second week of June, draw a picture of your perfect pet. It can be any kind of animal. You can even make up an animal of your own. Don't forget to give your pet a name and hang up your picture!

Words to Know

April—the fourth month of the year. It comes after March.
beak—the bill of a bird.
deserve—to be worthy or fit to receive a thing or award.
June—the sixth month of the year. It comes after May.

Web Sites

To learn more about May, visit ABDO Group online at **www.abdopublishing.com**. Web sites about May are featured on our Book Links page. These links are routinely monitored and updated to provide the most current information available.